Steps to Success

ISBN: 978-0-244-97055-0

Cover photo by Hmm360 courtesy of Morguefile.com

Contact Jack at
Jmallonsteps2success@gmail.com

Jack Mallon – Who am I?

A recent graduate. Here's my CV and some achievements:

September 2012 – August 2016 (University of Stirling, (1ˢᵗ Class) BA (Honours) History Degree)
- **First-class degree**
- Stirling Guildry Award for **Best History Dissertation** in a British or Scottish history topic (2016)
- **Best in class** for the module "Radicalism to labourism: popular politics, 1800-1914" (Spring semester 2015)
- **Best in class** for "The Golden Age of the Scottish Parliament. Parliament and Politics in Scotland, 1660-1707" (Special subject 2015-2016)
- Increased average from 63 in 3ʳᵈ year to 70 in 4ᵗʰ year.
- Sports editor at Brig Newspaper
- Sport's section awarded "Most Improved" by Brig committee in 2016.
- Member of lacrosse club between 2012 and 2014.

September 2016 – August 2017 (University of Stirling and Pompeu Fabra University (Barcelona), MSc in Strategic Communications and Public Relations)
- **Merit degree**
- 64% in Dissertation

Pompeu Fabra University:
- Worked on an anti-racism campaign "La Prueba Prejuicios"
- Edited the "La Prueba Prejuicios" campaign website and blog using Weebly.
- Worked as part of an integrated campaign with each specialist campaign team.

- Built a model campaign plan with a timeline and budget
- Built a non-profit advocacy campaign plan
- Conducted a research project on VisitScotland with interviews with listed business owners

Introduction

I had the idea to put my experience on paper after a number of good friends asked me about individual aspects of how to write better essays. Almost all students are looking to improve to some extent, but I could see that my friends were willing to work hard and be self-critical in order to do this. So I thought, wouldn't it be better to have everything in this one simple source that you can read in a few days?

I know that I can give insight on making considerable improvements over a short period of time. Aside from TIME the other important factor is EFFICIENCY! Making sure that the way you work translates into more marks gained and fewer wasted.

In order to increase my average from a 63 to a 70 in just over 12 months I had to locate and change the essential parts of my daily routine, research strategy, and working techniques. If you stick to the strategies in this book I know you too can improve your academic performance. It worked for me.

Jack Mallon

How to use this book.

Steps to Success can be read all in one go but you'll find that the tips and hints in this manual have been carefully designed to help students at those most intense points where things aren't working as they should.

For instance, if you are having problems keeping up with seminars, the best idea would be to flip to the CONTENTS page and look up chapters like *8 Ways to Take Full Advantage of Seminars.* Or maybe you are trying to improve your essay results. There's a chapter for that: *5 Essential Ways to Steal Back Marks on Essays.* The chapters are short but the work they suggest will take up lots of your time, so get ready for some hard graft.

Whether you are having trouble researching, writing, communicating or even struggling to make friends while studying, you'll find lots of easy to digest tips in this book which have been tried and tested and really work.

My advice would be to carry the book with you at all times, whether in the classroom, study group, seminar or library. When you hit a block there will be something in here to take you out of it so you can focus all your energies on upping those marks.

Good luck with your studies and let me know how you get on using the book. Like every good student I'm always open to good ideas.

Contents

Before we begin, here are three things which every first year student needs to do

First year. It's an exciting time. RIGHT?

Whether you're moving away from home, making new friends, have just turned 18, or all of the above, it is a massive step in each of our lives.

It is good to get the most from this experience and make a head start, because you are less likely to have the time in your remaining years – especially your dissertation year.

Each person has a different experience of university. I just want to share a few hints and tips from mine to help you take advantage of potential opportunities as soon as you can.

Join clubs

Membership in clubs and societies at university can provide you with critical experience for your future career. The occupational societies such as the political clubs, academic subject-specific clubs,

11

and media societies, are a clear example. However, in any society which is organised by its members and organises events or other activities throughout the year it is possible to gain valuable experience – especially if you are a committee member.

Joining clubs in your first year is very valuable because it gives you the opportunity to see how you fit it with different groups of people and different activities. It is important to test the ground in order to find clubs that are the right fit for you.

For example, I was a member of the drama society and two sports clubs in my first 2 years, so it took me a while to find the activity which I had real interest and passion for.

I joined the university newspaper in my third year, and became sports editor at the beginning of my fourth year. Even though I was at a disadvantage to the editors in that same position who had been writers since their first year, they were patient and showed me how to use the essential editing software. Likewise, I did the same for new writers to replace me.

So I am grateful to myself that I tried out other clubs in first and second year, because that allowed me to find out where my passion really lay.

Explore your new campus and new city

There are hidden gems on every campus. Especially, if you are in a new town or city the world is your oyster.

I couldn't wait to move away from home and gain my independence. However, it wasn't until the final month of my final year after I had submitted my dissertation that I really explored my campus at the University of Stirling. I had always thought of Stirling as a small campus in the middle of nowhere, but I then found a list online about the gems on my campus.

In the last two months before I moved out of my campus I had visited:
- a monument to one of Scotland's national heroes;
- a mountain peak overlooking the whole campus.

- the lake and fed the ducks and swans;
- several charming cafes and restaurants I had only every looked in and passed by.

Pro-actively make friendship gestures with your new flatmates

When you are living with new people it can be intimidating and even difficult to bond. In my first week at Stirling University I missed some major opportunities to bond with my flatmates when I didn't go out the first night. So I'm giving you this advice based on the steps I took to re-establish and reinforce positive relationships with my flatmates.

I took it upon myself to find out my flatmates' birthdays and also some more of their personal interests. That way I was able to personalise cards, gifts, and greetings.

In turn, it helped when I moved into new accommodation in each following year to learn from mistakes which were made.

1

Essays,
Seminars
and Exams

Top 8 ways to take full advantage of seminars.

After 5 years in University, I have spent more hours in seminars than I would care to calculate. Mastering seminars is about more than the small grade percentage you gain for attendance and contribution. If done properly, seminars can give you a decisive edge in gaining a 1st in both essays and exams.

The most important running factor is that you can spark creativity and critical thinking, and locate specific evidence or ideas easily without stressing.

However, even when you are discussing the most invigorating subject, at the right time of day, in a room which is close enough to a coffee source during break time, eventually you will feel like an impenetrable wall has built around your brain and you simply cannot take in anything else.

To prove that these techniques can work, I will show you how they worked for me under less than ideal circumstances.

In my final year we selected our extra module on the basis of ranking the seven topics on offer by preference (1 Most – 7 Least). I was given my 5th choice, in a module which **I was not initially attracted to or in any way knowledgeable about.**

My professor was a world-leading expert in the field, and not prone to giving the benefit of the doubt when mistakes were made, so there was no way I could shortcut my way through it or cut any corners or my marks would suffer.

Therefore, I am confident that if these 8 methods are applied consistently and correctly that you will be able to efficiently gather useful insights for your essays.

Overall Rules

1 ALWAYS keep an ideas sheet on the table

On the ideas sheet note any debates or questions which your tutor emphasises or hints at, because there's a good chance that **they could be your exam questions!**

Deal with the ideas sheet each week, and keep a separate list at the front of your folder for BIG IDEAS and QUESTIONS that you need time to work on or make use of.

2 Come to seminars with SPECIFIC questions on work you are doing or want to do.

When you want to find things out from your tutor it helps to articulate your questions precisely. For example, if you ask "How do I study better?" then your tutor can only give you a thin spread of advice across the board – bearing in mind that they will have dozens of students like you to deal with.

Instead you could ask them:

Can you recommend an efficient method for cross-referencing?

Can you recommend an academic source which conflicts with the main recommended text?

Can you suggest some extra primary sources in order to explore this topic in greater depth?

Now you're getting helpful answers.

3 Make clear distinctions between different notes

Over time notes can become cluttered, and can prove to be overwhelming when it comes time to study for exams or find specific information for an essay.

After a seminar if I thought my notes were too messy and cluttered then I would re-write them on my computer while the information was still fresh in my mind. It also meant that I could find specific gaps to fill in, and questions to put on the ideas sheet.

Increasing your Seminar Grade

4 Come prepared to contribute effectively to discussion

I spent the majority of my first two years doing the assigned reading because I had to. I did not think about how I could use my time and effort to effectively contribute to the group discussion. It was only in my final two years that I decided to make changes to my strategy for reading and note taking.

I would prepare a short summary of an assigned text. I would write 150 words because that was how much I could read out loud in 1 minute flat, which allowed me to reach the core of the argument decisively. This would also help me later on when I worked on my final 2 essays and prepared for my final exams.

If your seminar has a particular question or some focuses then make a list with some particular insights.

Essays

5 Select your essay questions in advance

Selecting an essay question in advance can allow you to take full advantage of seminars because you can focus your energy on establishing what you need to find out from your seminar, following useful leads to study before and after. This is a more productive method than focusing equally on every seminar and finding yourself short of time when the intense essay period begins.

In my final year, all history students were expected to write their own essay questions, to be approved by our supervisor. However, this strategy can also work if you are given a list of essay questions to choose from at the start of term.

6 Shortlist primary evidence to boost originality

If you know your essay topic, then you can keep a list of the relevant evidence presented in seminars with a note on why they are useful, so that you can work more efficiently and not waste so much time in examining evidence which cannot help your argument.

For more information on boosting your originality to achieve higher marks check out '*How Boosting my Originality Led to a First Class Degree*' on page 31

Exams

7 Ask your tutor about what to expect in the exams

This may seem obvious, but I have found myself in so many seminar groups where the students are afraid to ask the tutor in front of their peers about what things they can expect in the exam paper, such as **how many questions** there will be and **how many seminar topics** they should study.

I also found that when you discover where your exam will take place it can help your nerves to visit the room when it is empty. It meant that I worried a great deal less about the exam situation itself, and I could concentrate on my strategy for answering the different possible questions.

8 Write a summary of the main points each week, with an academic or primary source for each.

When the cramming gets underway, every minute counts towards memorising the evidence and arguments, and so it helps to have a strong platform which you have built in advance, so that you are not drowning in a clutter of notes which you will struggle to organise.

Even if you are half way through the year, it will be beneficial to force yourself to write a short summary of your previous seminars containing the main topics from each week. If possible list the important academic sources which were covered that day with the specific arguments or evidence that was discussed. The last one was very good for enhancing my memory of sources and their association with particular arguments.

Enhancing your memory of the association between sources and arguments is important when you have to adapt your argument to the questions that you are given in the exam.

How to read efficiently and overcome mental block

I have recently been asked by good friends "how do you read so quickly" and "does skim reading really work".

Well the truth is that efficient and effective reading for research does not come from concentrating on speed, and skim reading is only efficient when you are looking for something very small and particular, which means that you can ignore other things.

I used to read large number of sources with an open mind, just hoping that I would come across information and evidence that I would find helpful. Instead I would end up confused, side-tracked, and often defeated by mental block. The mental block that comes from reading lots of sources is facilitated by a lack of understanding of what you want to obtain from sources and how you will build on your existing knowledge.

What does efficient reading depend on?

From my experience of success and failure, I have concluded that efficient reading depends on 2 things:

1 The order of the sources that you read

The order of the sources matters because it allows you to develop your core knowledge with less disruption, and also build upon that core knowledge more easily. It is always best to start with the **most recent** secondary source, because it will contain the most up-to-date outline of the schools of thought on the central debates. If the most recent text is not sufficiently thorough, then find the most recent text which describes the main debates and schools of thought on a topic.

After reading the most recent source, read the most **important** texts which **it has referenced** to represent the different schools of thought. Then you can branch out into sources that provide supplementary analysis.

2 What you want to obtain from reading a source

Once you have read two or three core texts in-depth I would then read my remaining texts with a clear aim in mind. Ask yourself – what am I looking to find out from this text? If it's in one of the prominent publications from one of the schools of thought, then look for what **evidence** has made them reach these conclusions.

Also, if it is a journal article, then look at the **summary paragraph** and the specific wording of the title at the beginning. If it is a book then take careful note of the specific wording of the chapter title. They will tell you about the specific focus and theory in the article so that you can develop a clear aim about what you want to find out from this text and how it will most likely fit in to your own assessment.

Some Extra Practical Tips

Read the Introduction Chapter of books

This is especially important for **literature reviews**, but it was also very useful for me when I worked on essays.

If you really want to understand the perspective of the authors then the **Introduction** is an ideal place to start. The author will outline how they have been influenced by previous research and how their research deviated from their predecessors.

Colour coding

Colour coding was a genuine life-saver for me when reading and making notes.

There are a vast number of ways to use colour-coding. For example, when I was trying to separate something from the rest of my notes, such as a cross-reference with another source of evidence, then colour-coding would make it very easy to find a piece of evidence later when you are tired or in a hurry.

Also, if you are looking through a large source of evidence, then you can use a few colours to identify your core categories.

However, do not be tempted to colour code anything that you think might be relevant. I found that there were few things more overwhelming and de-motivating that staring at a wall of colour on a page, with no more idea of what specific item was important than if there were no more colours that black and white on the page.

Top 5 essential tips for stealing back marks on essays

During my first three years at University I became accustomed to seeing people who seemed to put in less work than me, and yet achieved higher marks.

However, I am happy to tell you that there are things you can do to make your hard work worth that little bit extra, and to remove any excuse which the marker has to deduct points from your final grade. Remember that your marker could be looking through dozens of papers, and when confronted with faults which can only be judged subjectively the risk of the marker judging you harshly is increased tremendously.

In my final year, when I looked into the marking process and reviewed my feedback from previous years, I realised that I had been missing out on a large number of marks all these years. I bring this news to you in the hope that you also don't miss out.

Don't start with the largest source. Start with the most recent:

I found it very tempting to always start with the largest and most comprehensive academic source. I hoped to get it out of the way and get a wide overview from the start. However, one tutor advised me to start with the most recent source instead for one simple reason:

–it could inform you of the most recent schools of thought and trends in that particular area.

Even a small journal article can give you an overview of the opinions which have previous been put forward on the subject as well as a key list of sources in its bibliography. Since it is smaller than the comprehensive source it can also give you an simpler idea of the timeline of academic progression in your topic in a shorter period of time.

It also means that you can be more selective when studying the comprehensive source. Rather than trying to absorb all the information which you will then pick and chose from later, you can look for information of particular aspects of your topic.

Have an "outsider" take a look

By an "outsider" I mean someone who does not study your subject. The primary value in being reviewed by such a person is that they will not feel bound up by the specific criteria of excellence in your particular subject.

Instead they can focus on other things which can win or lose you marks such as spelling, grammar, the logical flow of the essay, and how easy it is to understand the your central argument. If a non-expert can easily track the flow of your argument then an expert marker certainly will.

Also, if you make the flow of your argument and presentation of evidence easy to track then your marker will be very grateful. Remember that they could be marking submitted projects from dozens of students in a week.

Have an "insider" take a look

On the flip side an "insider" (someone who does the same subject) can provide some helpful insight on the specific criteria which can influence grades specifically in your topic. I arranged on a number of occasions to review someone's' essay in exchange for them reviewing mine. Ideally ask someone who is working on a different area to yourself so that neither of you are tempted to copy.

Some of the best ideas I received on essays came from other students (including non-history students) who could suggest useful insights because they were not so invested in my specific topic and could examine it from a simpler viewpoint.

Look for essay assistance on campus

It was not until the final year of my undergraduate degree that I paid attention to the memos at the start of the year from the faculty manager. Far down the page he mentioned the services of a "Literary Fellow" for the department 3 days a week. After further inquiry, I realised that this "Literary Fellow" was a virtual miracle worker for those like me who work hard on research, but found the essay writing process exhausting and only saw weak results which did not reflect the measure of the work put into the essay.

In exchange for my hard work, I finally found someone who would point me in the right direction. I made an appointment several weeks in advance, because of the demands on the literary fellow's time, and when I went along to the meeting I realised that by utilising the language and essay structure properly it was possible to improve the presentation of your argument, regardless of your subject.

Look at previous dissertations for the topic

This is especially important for dissertation students, but can also be employed for other projects.

Firstly, it was difficult when faced with the scale of the dissertation to imagine how it would finally turn out and how much ground had to be covered. However, at the University of Stirling the dissertations which were awarded a Distinction were all available in the library. Just by glancing through them I was able to put my mind at ease about the presentation of my dissertation, because I knew then what features I had to include which were different from previous essays and how they would look.

Secondly, undergraduate dissertations are one of the most neglected areas of original academic insights in higher education. So if you can read dissertations related to your research topic which were awarded a Distinction in either your own university, or in other universities, then you will have access to fresh insights which may not even have caught on in peer reviewed academic journals.

How boosting my originality led to a first-class degree

In the final year of my undergraduate degree I was desperate to make the jump to first-class. I asked one of my previous tutors about the different between a second and a first-class essay. She said:

"A second-class essay is controlled by other peoples' insights on the evidence. A first-class essay is controlled by YOUR insights on the evidence … with help from secondary sources of course …"

In terms of assessing the evidence to add creative original insights while making a cohesive argument throughout your introduction, main section and conclusion, the most important factor is to embrace the exceptions to any overarching answer. It is crucial to acknowledge the gaps in the evidence, which limit your certainty about a conclusion.

That is why **originality** is such a bonus if you want to improve your grades. In this article I will explain why originality is useful, the best consistent methods of making original insights, and an example from my highest scoring essay to show how these methods work in practice.

How to make creative original insights

It can sound intimidating when thinking about making original ideas. For my first three years I did my best to understand the arguments of the recommended texts and cram them into the maximum word count.

However, it is much easier to be original than you think. I would spark my creativity after I had examined a primary source by writing the first 5 things about the subject which popped into my mind. Even if they did not seen relevant initially, putting them down on paper could lead me to another creative thought and spark new ideas which would support and enhance my argument.

Methods of making original creative insights

When you see the conclusions made in an article, look at the primary evidence that the authors have used, because primary evidence or raw data has to be the fundamental basis for any strong argument. It is the primary evidence which allows you to show that you understand the arguments that have previously been put forward or that your original argument has genuine substance to it.

Of course the first place to look for a list of primary data sources should be in your **course handbook**. However, you can also find the name of the evidence in the footnotes on the page, at the end of the chapter, or at the end of the book.

If the most useful sources of primary data are online then perfect. However, it is still worthwhile to look though the university library database. This allows you to find related evidence. If you cannot locate the primary sources in your own university library or archives then try typing in the author's name or the people described in the primary evidence into your University library database.

Now it would be a marathon task for a student to study the same amount of primary evidence for an essay that an academic would for an article. But you do not have to. All that you need is to have sufficient grounds on which to challenge or reinforce conclusions

Example from my experience

In my final essay as an undergraduate at Stirling University in February 2016 I had to write about how rival Protestant denominations affected party politics in the pre-1707 Scottish Parliament.

However, it became clear that party politics in the pre-1707 Scottish Parliament was too fluid to categorise absolutely and so I could not simply assign a YES or NO answer.

I employed the techniques shown above, which would allow me to cite rival academics work and critically challenge and reinforce some of their claims and take control of my argument.

The one thing which I could clarify was that in the specific time period that I was researching was that rivalry between Protestant denominations was consistently present. However, in order to answer the question properly I had to acknowledge how it fitted in with other factors which divided voting parliamentarians into rival factions.

I listed the occasions where rival Protestant factions actually broke ranks, and read over the list to categorise what factors were most frequent and what exactly would compel large numbers of parliamentarians to vote with rival Protestant factions – which was most frequently the **threat of violence** from government forces or the **financial benefits** of a royal pension.

So instead of saying that rival protestant denominations were the most important factor in party politics, I used the evidence that I had gathered to show that it was a **consistent** factor which was only broken by certain **exceptional** events.

Top 8 tips for improving your dissertation

My dissertation finally finished on a wet and windy day. I had submitted it two months previously and began research on it thirteen months before that, but finally I got to hold it proudly – along with my first-class degree and my Stirling Guildry Award for highest awarded score in a British or Scottish history topic.

A few key tactics had a tremendous influence on how successful my dissertation was in thoroughly covering the subject area.

I will share them with you now.

Wording of your dissertation title

In late January 2016, I was faced with finalising the final wording of my official dissertation title. Some of my peers were not so concerned with this seemingly innocuous task when there seemed to be far more important jobs to do.

But be under no illusions, the most critical factor in gaining a higher mark in any piece of work is that you **answer the question**. So you must look at the scope of the evidence you have obtained, and can obtain in the future, and decide where to set the boundaries of your topic. Therefore, the wording of your dissertation can make the difference between a comprehensive assessment and an almost-comprehensive assessment.

Cultivate a strong relationship with your supervisor

Although you have to conduct the research and writing yourself, your supervisor plays an essential role in guiding you in the right direction. Remember that they will have seen the mistakes made by students before and will be able to help you to avoid the pitfalls that have caught out previous students.

I met several of my peers who were so concerned about being a nuisance to their supervisor or stepping over boundaries that they emailed them less than 10 times during the entire dissertation period.

Even if you do contact your supervisor too much, or overstep some boundary, that is always better than coming to them too little. The last thing your supervisor wants is for your dissertation to stall or fall apart.

The best advice I can give for getting the answers you want from a busy supervisor is to send one email with the precise questions which you have built up during a research or writing session. If that means keeping an email draft and then sending it off in time for your supervisor to answer the next day, well then it is still more helpful then keeping silence.

Make each chapter cohesive and absolutely related to your question:

Keep a one paragraph thesis statement about what exactly you are trying to prove in your research. Then you can make a similar thesis for each of your chapters, (or different sections of each of your research chapters), so it becomes easier to appreciate the logical flow of your argument and which parts need to be altered or filled in with extra evidence or analysis.

Cross-reference the evidence for guidance

Cross-referencing evidence is what allows you to successfully compose a strong argument. If you haven't done so already, then take your largest source of evidence and **highlight** the patterns which emerge that are relevant to the debate you are concentrating on.

Once you have started with the largest source of evidence then it will be easier to use the smaller ones to reinforce or contradict your findings from the first source.

When you infer something in a pattern after cross-referencing evidence then you should write it as a chunk of text, with the evidence included, which you can then cut and paste into your dissertation. This is a great solution to writer's block.

After completing this process what I ended up with were large Word Documents – easy to find on my computer, pen drives, and Google Drive – which contained the original notes I had taken as well as clearly distinguished small paragraphs with conclusions that I could cut and paste into my dissertation. Then I could supplement and alter them based on evidence which I came across in other sources.

Look at primary data sources outside the immediate location

If you are able to examine your debate from a greater variety of perspectives then you will be more likely to take control of the evidence.

For example, my history dissertation was focused on the unique success of the Independent Labour Party in Glasgow after 1931, which did not occur in any other location. However, due to the small amount of surviving materials which relate only to the Independent Labour Party in Glasgow, I searched for other perspectives, such as materials on the national Independent Labour Party as well as local Glasgow branches of rival political parties.

In addition to looking at the Mitchell Library's extensive collections on the Glasgow branches, I visited the London School of Economics, the Peoples' History Museum in Manchester, the Scottish Labour History Society, Local History Groups in Glasgow, the National Library of Scotland in Edinburgh, as well as online archives such as British Newspapers, 1600-1950.

I always emailed archivists in advance for their recommendations. This was a crucial tactic for me in scraping back extra marks onto my final grade, because I was able to locate evidence which had only arrived days before and was not listed on the official records yet.

Ask experts in the field about the most up-to-date texts

Once you locate the most comprehensive or recent texts on your particular topic area, or related to a particular part of your topic area, it is a good idea to contact the author to ask them about their opinion on what is the most comprehensive and up-to-date research on the topic. It will be easy enough to locate their email address on their university profile page. Make sure that you state your exact question and area of study, because they might be able to tell you some more specific useful texts in addition to answering your specific question.

Double and triple check your references and bibliography

The referencing and final bibliography might seem relatively unimportant, and it is for that exact reason why many people waste good marks by neglecting it. A dissertation which has taken you months can be read by your marker in less than an hour, so it will not be difficult for them to notice mistakes in the referencing.

If you have a referencing guide for your subject, then by the time you have submitted your dissertation you should know it off my heart. Some things to look out for are whether your in-text references or footnotes and supposed to be the same as in your bibliography, and what they expect you to write as a reference if you are citing the same source more than once.

Give your dissertation to both an "outsider" and an "insider" for review:

I became so accustomed to my own writing style that I would miss obvious mistakes. If possible, have your work read by different people. It serves different benefits to have your work looked over by an "outsider", meaning someone who hasn't studied your subject, and an "insider", meaning someone who has.

An outsider will be able to analyse the more acute points related to your subject. An insider will focus more on the spelling and grammar, and will also be able to advise you if it is overly elaborate and confusing. However, be careful to select an insider who is not studying the same area as you, so that neither of you are tempted to adjust your own work based on the other persons' work.

How to carefully manage your research for a first-class degree

The most important factor for me in obtaining a first-class degree was in learning how to manage my research more efficiently.

The spider-web management strategy was absolutely critical to turning my ordinary academic performance into a first-class degree, because it allowed me to catch as many good ideas and pieces of evidence as possible.

Problems with other strategies

In any large project the potential to be overwhelmed is constant. On many large projects, I found that after taking notes on over a dozen sources, and running across dozens of scenarios in my head, that my final submission would not include the majority of them, and that the extra reading had only served to confuse me and disrupt the coherence of my arguments.

When I was in creative beast mode and there were a seemingly infinite number of ideas on my work flying in at once, it was necessary to have a system where I could focus on the flow of my reading or writing, and record my different ideas while not getting side-tracked.

I had previously employed two methods of researching and then writing an essay or presentation. Firstly, to research enough that I could write a first draft and complete further research and drafting until I could complete my final version.

My second system was to research until I had written an essay plan which I was confident with and then write a single draft.

I found that both of those methods brought different problems that handicapped my ability to build a strong cohesive argument.

Instead, I embraced ORGANISED CHAOS.

Spider-web strategy

First and foremost, the spider-web strategy requires the individual to be committed to thorough research. Commitment in this context refers to the hours which are invested in work over days at a time, as well as the discipline to complete specific tasks each day.

I especially needed the four things listed below, in order to keep my essay research on course and efficiently capture my most creative ideas, build an ideal structure, and from that build a cohesive thread of argument that fitted with the evidence which I had for each section of the topic:

Ideas Sheet

In every major research-based project that I will ever undertake I will use an ideas sheet.

You can use it to articulate an aspect of the direction that your project is taking, for example: what a piece of evidence could prove, what different pieces of evidence combined could prove, and what specific evidence you should look for later.

In previous projects I had written pages and pages of notes, and found some cracking pieces of evidence, but when I was writing the essay I would have to look through this massive pile of notes to find each individual piece at the point where I thought they would be useful. That is why the ideas sheet made such a difference in translating my hard work into increased marks.

First Draft

I used a first draft to write lumps of text that could be transferred directly into my final draft.

When I was reading and researching, if I felt that I knew how a particular point could be written then I would write it in my first draft, rather than making notes and risking the possibility that I would suffer from writer's block when I began writing my final draft.

This had an immediate impact in my final year because I had previously had a serious problem with reaching even the minimum work count. If you can go above the maximum word count, while giving yourself sufficient time to edit it down, then you will be able to produce a more refined piece of work.

Thesis Statement

A thesis statement is essentially another ideas sheet, specifically for directing your project's overall argument.

I would make a thesis statement at the beginning of a project, and re-appraise or add to it each day that I was working on the project. It was critical for providing direction to the project and ensuring that I not waste a lot of time studying and working with information that was not useful for the direction of my essay.

When you review the ideas sheet and first draft at the end of every day the natural following step is to make any necessary adaptations to your thesis statement.

'Civil Engineering' deadlines

My dissertation supervisor gave me great inspiration with a story about his experience as a PhD student. In order to managing the large and chaotic work load, he planned writing his final PhD manuscript along the metaphorical lines of a **civil engineering** project.

In civil engineering, it is necessary to split projects up into the most essential core tasks that have separate deadlines. So put these tasks first and assign separate deadlines for each of them, and if there are extra things that you would like to do that could boost your grade, then set time aside each day or in the final days before your deadline for "Extra Tasks" where you can do as many of these as possible.

Stages to fulfill every day

Essential Core Tasks (Reading specific sources, writing particular sections, and reviewing certain aspects of our project):

(Note): I know that this seems like a lot however I must add that I would spend 80 – 90% of my time on the Essential Core Tasks. The only purpose of the other four tasks is to increase the efficiency of the Essential Core Tasks and increase your marks.

Extra Core Tasks

- Review your Ideas Sheet
- Read over the chunks of text in your first draft
- Review your Thesis Statement
- Update your 'Civil Engineering' Deadlines.

Necessary PowerPoint presentation skills for university

Public speaking can seem very intimidating. To deliver a comprehensive argument to your peers with time racing past you was never designed to be on our easy-to-do lists.

Delivering a first-class presentation is based around 2 major overarching factors: speaking style and delivery, and the content of the presentation and the strength of your argument. Using these steps you will be in a strong position to showcase your best work when delivering a PowerPoint.

Practice speaking and amend the presentation to improve delivery

This is the most prominent area of preparation where neglecting delivery in favour of content could potentially cost you extra marks.

A well worded argument on paper can sound awkward when spoken directly, so you should always practice speaking and note which parts should be amended so that they still reflect your core argument but allow you deliver it smoothly in your speech.

Also structure the speech to reflect the practical aspects of delivering a presentation, including the times when you change slides and hand out visual aids.

Don't be over-reliant on printed notes with exact wording
The key to a successful presentation is that you understand your argument so well that you can describe it naturally without having to rely on a script. It is good for the audience to connect with you, which makes eye-contact essential and dependence on a script to be counter-productive. Likewise, if you try to remember all your words exactly then it will not sound natural to the audience, because a good description sounds very different on paper than it does in a real speech.

This will also be helpful if you are asked questions after the presentation is completed.

The 1 – 5 method for confident posture and poise
When I used to stand before an audience I would shiver and shake just enough to distract people from the argument that I was trying to make. That was before I learned the 1 -5 technique for maintaining a calm posture and poise in front of my audience.

Before speaking just take a deep breath and imagine a semi-circle with 5 levels on it (with 1 as lowest and 5 as highest) inside your body which controls your energy and confidence. If you are nervous before a presentation then imagine you are on level 2. Every time you breathe out imagine that you are going up a level. Keep going until you imagine yourself at level 5.

It has been scientifically proven that focusing on your breathing can allow us to take a step back from our thoughts and regain control of our concentration, which allows us to feel more calm and composed.

Speak as if the most important people are at the back of the room

When you are concerned primarily with the content in your argument it is easy to neglect the delivery. I have on occasionally spoken so quietly and quickly that some of the audience did not understand the argument made in my presentation.

So I picture a single person in the very back of the room and I speak as if I was only addressing them.

Resist the temptation to deviate from a text-based presentation

PowerPoint presentations can be very colourful, with a lot of pretty groovy graphics. However, the people who are watching and listening to your presentation want to understand the essence of your argument, and while images and videos can help convey your points and make them entertaining they must always remain an addition to your core evidence.

If some members of the audience are taking notes then they will appreciate it if you have written some explanation of your points so that they can take photos or just quick notes.

Write a full list of citations

Please resist the temptation to be grudging with your referencing because it is a presentation.

According to my tutor's reports, my tutor rewarded me for the "strong foundations of your argument, which could be easily referenced back to your sources".

Having a text-based presentation also gives you're an opportunity to showcase your thorough research and preparation, including in-text referencing throughout the slides ('source/date' or 'source/part of title/date' if necessary).

50

Five tips for perfect referencing for essays

As a history student "Referencing" became one of those nasty buzzwords which I associated with losing marks regardless of the quality of my argument. However, correct referencing is essential for validating all references, and with these 5 necessary tips you will stay on top of your referencing and not lose any extra marks.

I have used the Harvard System, the Chicago system, and the specific Stirling History systems of referencing. The tips which I will give you today will be applicable for all referencing strategies, with the common condition that the reader is aiming to be absolutely thorough in their referencing.

Cite in-text immediately

The most important tip is when you've written a point containing evidence is to cite the evidence immediately, while it is still in your head.

The biggest mistake which I made with referencing was to say that I would do it when my essay was finished. My style of researching, writing and editing meant that I never finished before that day that an assignment was due.

If you balance the interesting tasks with the more mundane tasks then it will all work out a lot easier.

Cite in bibliography immediately

If you have cited a source in-text or in a footnotes then immediately put it into your bibliography or check to see that it has already been put in.

Also double check when you are finished that every source included in your in-text citations or footnotes has been put in your bibliography. I have missed a few at the last minute before and been penalised, for the mistake and for the sheer obviousness with which the marker could spot it.

Use keyword search on your PC (#lifesaver):

Hit ctrl + f on the keyboard of your PC and it will allow you to search for and locate every use of any letter, number, or symbol, as well as combinations of all of them. It was recommended to me by my friend Liam and it is a lifesaver when you are double crossing references for spelling, style, and composition.

If your referencing system requires you to have a shorter version of the reference after the first time that you cite it, then this will allow you to locate the first time that a particular source has been cited.

An added benefit of this system is that it allows you to notice if you've cited two articles the same way (e.g. Smith, 2016). It is quite common for a prolific academic or an academic with a common surname to have multiple texts in one year. Then check how your referencing system specifies how to distinguish them.

Double-check when you use referencing software

If you use referencing software such as RefWorks then do not make the mistake of assuming that you can rely on it 100%. Always review it afterwards with a study guide.

Stick to ONE referencing guide

For my undergraduate degree, all history students were fortunate enough to be given a style guide by the department. As long as we studied and stuck to the rules contained within it we would not lose any marks from it.

However, for my postgraduate degree we were told what style to use and to find a guide ourselves, even though the most popular guides on the particular referencing style were incomplete. But the important condition which we were all given was that the referencing style should be consistent throughout an individual essay, which would mean that we were not penalised, except for major errors.

Ultimate strategy to ace your exams

The strategy which I'm about to tell you about comes from years and years of trying to excel in exams and finally acing them in my final semester as an undergraduate.

My previous strategies had failed because of a lack of hours invested in preparation, or by attempting to learn everything as a bundle of information for each subject, or by trying to prepare a perfect answer without sufficient room for adaptability.

Filing Cabinet System

A well organised and detailed filing cabinet system is the perfect metaphor for preparing for exams.

A high-quality filing cabinet system will contain all of the information, but will also have a log of where exactly each piece of information is contained and the order in which the information is stored. Likewise I would prepare for history exams by memorising information on four or five topics which could come up in a logical order so that I would be able to cover the topic fully in my answer.

How to prepare for your exams

Just like organising a filing cabinet, you have to account for all of the information first.

I would read my seminar notes and then outline and read particular texts for the topic from each seminar week in order to build up a structure for a possible question.

Starting with a basic structure with the logical order of events, I would build up the skeleton with notes of useful academic sources with some details on their stance and research, and then boil it down to just the sub-sections and sources.

This where putting the hours in matters! I would memorise both lists at the same time so that I would instinctively know the details, but I would have a minimised version in my head as well so that I could have an overview from where I could pick and choose what details I needed to add in, based on the exact question that came up in the exam.

What are the benefits for students?

The main benefit of this system for me was that I wasted less time pondering all of the information which I had crammed in the week before. Instead I had boiled everything down to some key points, and when I then focused on any one of them it would immediately unlock the information on authors, dates, and arguments.

Although you are remembering the individual points for each topic in a particular order, using this system also allows you to mix into a different order if the essay question requires you to.

Extra considerations

Get into a good sleeping pattern

When I say put the hours in do not be tempted to work past the hours when your mind is actually learning anything. Another major difference in my preparation for exams in my final year was that I had been able to sort out my sleeping routine so that I was always in bed before 10:30pm and always out of bed before 7:30am.

Work in groups

I met up with some members of my seminar group in the three weeks leading up to the exams. We would each bring our notes on our individual assigned texts to share so that each of us were not having to read everything, and compete with each other for the limited number of copies in the library. We would also work on building a skeleton plan on each topic together for mutual benefit.

Achieve any ambition through careful mapping

This might be an appropriate topic for mid-year, the time when your ideal visions may be wearing down. How do you make plans that you can stick to?

As someone with considerable experience in making overstretched plans I know how it is easy to give up on plans when you do not see how the end target can be reached.

Why a heavy workload has benefited my quality of life

First of all I want to emphasise why embracing a heavy workload has actually been better for my day-to-day quality of life and happiness.

Having a lot to do has benefited me in a number of ways.

I now have motivation to force myself to give up bad habits. For example, as a teenager I would watch YouTube almost every night until the small hours of the morning, even when I got bored though I knew that just one more video would be enough ... but it rarely was!

However, I also knew that I am not a productive night-time worker, which meant that my first step towards productivity and better results had to be an early night sleep so that I could realistically wake up early in the morning.

Being preoccupied brings me a great sense of contentment outside of University. At school my main concern was socialising, with work being an extra thing to do. Even in my first year at University, I was still only planning for the next few months at a time without thinking about my long-term ambitions. However, after graduation there are no more excuses and mapping my ambitions has encouraged me to pursue even more ambitious goals than the ones that I was already working on.

How to make your ambitions reachable

The biggest reason for the failure of any ambition is that it lacks a unit of measurement.

The most popular resolutions I've heard so far in 2018 are related to fitness or weight loss or going back to gym. However, few people I've met have put a practical measurement on any of these ambitions.

My personal fitness resolution for this year is to run at least one half-marathon and one marathon. These ambitions will push me to increase the number of times I run each week and how long I spend on each run, because I know from experience how painful a long-competitive run can be when I've not prepared my body or my mind for the experience.

Also I have seen a lot of people become disturbed by the lack of control which they have over the long-term circumstances in their life. So I have coped with this by setting it as an ultimate goal and setting measurable goals that will set the ground to receive better opportunities.

For example, you might say that I want to find a job in the next five years where I am earning over £30,000/year. However, you are not certain if a promotion will be available in your own organisation or how many such jobs will be available in such companies. Therefore, the actual goal has to be to network in order to be in a good position to hear about and get the insight on, and qualify for the job you will seek in the future, and secondly to stay up-to-date will the trends in your job sector – especially those which are useful for someone in the position you hope that you will obtain.

For any ambitions related to personal relationships the main features, such as showing affection and building trust are harder to quantify and measure. So what you have to do is translate it into real actions. Having just left university, all of my friends have moved home, so I now make a point of speaking to friends on Facebook who I have not spoken to for a while. Sometimes that is all that is needed to reinforce a good friendship.

Time management and managing conflicting priorities in your final semester

Time management! After you graduate from university it will still be a big buzzword, with a large amount of relevance to your academic and professional success and development.

When I struggled with a large project my instinct was to persist and eventually I would break it down to the point where I was satisfied and could concentrate on other projects. However, this led to severe neglect of smaller tasks and the loss of a large number of marks.

What I have learned from my final year, as well as my postgraduate degree and job applications to large organisations, is that there are 4 steps which have to be taken when organising your priorities.

What is the scale of what is being done?

List the tasks which you are undertaking in order of the scale of the workload. By workload, I mean the size of the final submission, the amount of research involved, and the percentage of marks allocated to the particular task out of your final degree or module grade. This will allow you to prioritize the tasks that you will have to do if you are planning ahead.

My weekly planner (which you can find on my website) is based on the plan that I had in my final semester. You can see that I have committed some time every week in order to maintain progression in my dissertation, while splitting other tasks depending on which week it was due.

It is important to consider what you are aiming for when you undertake a task. For example, as a history student I wanted to locate some useful primary sources to reinforce my argument, but if I already had evidence that could reinforce a particular point, then I would prioritise other tasks first, and only search for evidence when I had finished these other essential tasks..

Also, if you are looking through a large source of secondary or primary evidence to be aware before of what you are looking to find out, because that will help you decide how much time you should spend looking at that source. For example, when I read through election results in Glasgow parliamentary constituencies between 1918 and 1945 I kept an eye out for 3 things:

Each year, how many constituencies did the Independent Labour Party contest without Labour Party endorsement?

Each year, how many constituencies did the Independent Labour Party win?

Each year, of the constituencies that the Independent Labour Party won, how many where against a Labour Party and/or a Communist Party candidate?

By following the advice above it will be possible for you to measure the scale of what you need to do, and assign your time appropriately, so that you will get the most out of your work, and hopefully boost your grade.

Who is it being done for?

The person or group that the tasks is being completed for is important, because it gives you an alternative form of setting precedence for tasks in case, for example, you have multiple tasks with a similar size and importance, or if the deadlines are close together. You can consider exactly what the person or group that you are delivering the task for wants and how they will grade you on it. How much extra time will you need to familiarize yourself with the equipment or techniques that will be necessary to complete the task to the highest possible standard?

For example, in my dissertation I had to complete other parts to the physical paper that was submitted then I would for an ordinary essay. So I assigned extra time to add each of these in, so that I would not lose marks.

For example, if you are not comfortable with giving presentations then it would be very beneficial for you to schedule some time giving practice presentations so that you become more comfortable with your speaking and the practical issues which you will face when using PowerPoint. (See page 47 for tips on PowerPoint presentations)

What do I need to get in order to complete the task?

Do any of your tasks require you wait in order to get something from another person? If so, schedule when you have to contact them, when you expect to receive the thing, and when you will do if it does not arrive on time.

For example, when I was in my final year I was also sports editor of the student newspaper "Brig". More than other sections, sport had to be focused on stories from the previous week. This meant that our coverage and writing would be based primarily in one week of the month, and so during the rest of the month I could focus on other tasks.

Also, this is very important if you are working as part of a group. When you are assigned team members for a group assignment you must be very clear about the steps that you have to take in order to complete the assignment and the number and scope of the sections of work which you will have to complete for the final assignment.

For group work, the first step is to develop a work plan based on the following factors:

- Agree on meeting times for initial discussion, joint study sessions, and for putting the final assignment together;
- Agree who will complete the different parts of the final assignment;
- Make sure that each team member is completely aware of their responsibilities;
- Make sure that you all understand the thread of argument which you have put together. This is especially important for presentations.

If the schedule doesn't go to plan?

Even the best plans can come undone, and being productive can mean combining strict organisation with some necessary flexibility. So always be prepared to do other pieces of work during the time which you have set aside for a particular task just in case you cannot work on it.

For example, in April 2016 I had to finish my final essay, my final presentation, and the final draft of my dissertation. So I scheduled my time according to steps 1 and 3. One morning when I was supposed to be working with my partner on the final presentation, after 10 minutes of waiting for him at the library, he texted me to say that he could not make it until the afternoon. Thankfully I brought another small folder containing my most essential dissertation notes so that I would not waste hours doing nothing.

The 5 essential lifestyle changes for improving academic performance

To start us off, it is important to understand that success on any level will be influenced by our day-to-day lifestyle. All of the events and features of our life are interconnected insofar as they impact on how we think and what we think about, both of which deeply impact on our productivity.

Now I must emphasise that these are ideal scenarios. Like most of you I will fall short in seeking perfection. Please do not let this discourage you, for even aspiring to commit fully to these lifestyle choices each day had a beneficial impact on my living standard and academic performance. Also make sure that you adjust this to what suits you. I merely provide these examples to show how I adjusted my living habits to optimise my living standards.

1: Work out your peak hours

We all have times of the day when we work at our best. Where we feel more relaxed, and able to focus and comprehend complex information and create our best original insights.

When you want to work hard it can sometimes lead to hours of working during your bad hours when you feel like you're banging your head off a brick wall, because even the hardest working and most ambitious person needs a decent sleep (ideally 8 hours) to rejuvenate their creative spark.

As I am a morning person I adjusted my schedule towards getting into the library between 8:00 – 8:30 every morning, and set my hardest tasks first in the schedule. This was difficult considering that I habitually watched YouTube until 1 – 2 in the morning. So I would switch off all electronic devices before leaving the library to stave off the YouTube and Facebook craving, and I would only switch them back on to set my alarm when I was finally relaxed enough to sleep, which was usually about 9:30.

I would then pack my bag for the next day, pile up the clothes which I would wear, pack a bag with my lunch (with fruit and water) and leave it in the fridge.

The whole purpose of working out peak working hours and setting up a routine for the beginning and end of the day is to remove unnecessary chaos from our lives, so we can focus on what matters most.

2: Exercise

Have you ever found yourself feeling completely restless, unable to concentrate on your work, and taking break after break simply because you feel so uncomfortable sitting down. Then you are in need of exercise.

At the same time that I was conducting research for my dissertation and other subjects, I was training for the Great Scottish Run half-marathon. This allowed me to stay focused and gave me a reason to go running regularly.

However, the most important criteria for exercising is realising when it would be helpful. Just like when you work out your peak hours, you should try to be aware of what times of the day you feel restless and unable to concentrate fully on your work. At this time you should try different types of exercise to see what suits you.

Whether it is a 15 minute walk outside the library, or a long run, or training with a sports team, it will benefit you in so many ways to burn off some physical energy and refocus your mind.

3: Bring healthy food to the library

During my last all-night writing session for my final 4000 word essay, I had a remarkable déjà vu moment. Opposite me was a 2nd year with 3 empty and 3 full cans of red bull – a traditional fuel for staying awake for long hours.

I on the other hand brought a bundle of 7 bananas. I had begun bringing fruit for study ever since I drunk 5 red bulls in my 3rd year only to find that I still couldn't resist napping, and when I did work I couldn't articulate or process information well enough to produce high-quality work.

Bananas on the other hand gave me a longer slow-release burst of energy, which was for more suited to a late night or all night work session.

Important Note
In addition to fruit, it is important to keep hydrated by drinking water.

An occasional caffeine pickup is still acceptable. If the coffee shops have all closed, and you don't like what the machine gives you, then invest in a flask. I paid as much for one flask as **2 coffees** from Starbucks would have cost me, so the financial benefits should act as an extra incentive.

4: Alter social media habits

I used social media every day during my final year at University. So I am not going to lie through my teeth by telling you to give it up.

Instead it will benefit you if you alter your social media habits so that they do not distract you during your peak working hours.

In the morning, I would not check social media at all, so that I was not dwelling on it during peak working hours. I would just check my emails, they were often concerned with work and would put my mind at ease once I had dealt with them.

In the afternoon, during my lunch break, I would then answer all my social media messages and check my updates, because it was a good way to zone out of work for 45 minutes.

5: Use a calendar

Time management can be a super-power for an ambitious and successful individual. To maximise what you accomplish over the course of any period of time, using a calendar will give you the ultimate control to make sure nothing is missed and every task you face can be optimised.

Using a calendar for time management allows you to ensure that you can record opportunities at a future date, space out that tasks in front of you so that they can be realistically accomplished, and put your mind at ease if, like me, you crave control in the different aspects of your life.

I always used the android calendar app, because it would remind you even if you forgot to check your schedule, which made it better for me than a paper calendar or diary.

Maximise your time and achieve more

Time is our most precious asset. Once it's gone you cannot get it back, and yet it seems so easy to waste it. Ironically a lot of time is wasted fretting over how we should use our time.

There are simply not enough hours in the day to keep up with the tasks we set ourselves.

There are simply not enough months in the year to achieve all our resolutions.

There may not even be enough years in our lifetimes to see all that we want to!

But there is a solution! The key factors in effective time management are What, When, Who, and How.

In this chapter, I will show you real life examples of how you can manage your time using these four simple categories.

What, When, Who, and How

These four categories are essential for compressing your time. Compressing essential means that you take the opportunity to accomplish more tasks by using your circumstances to your advantage. Each of the four categories below is useful for isolating when is an appropriate time to work on a particular task, which in turn can leave you spare time to divide among your primary tasks as you so choose.

What do I need to finish this work?

What physical things are needed to complete this work? This is essential because you will save yourself a lot of time pondering lots of other factors which are not genuinely important. When you isolate what things are required then you now have a list of simple steps with which you can plan your immediate progress.

For example, if you need to analyse certain sources in order to complete an assignment then setting aside time to obtain and analyse each of them is a necessary step to take before completing the final draft of your assignment.

When would it be possible to do this work?

If you are doing work that has to be done during a certain time frame then you can isolate when you need to complete other tasks.

This is particularly useful when you have consistent working hours, or even if you find out your working hours for each week.

For example, when I was in my final undergraduate year I balanced my dissertation, with other academic assignments, with my position as the sports editor for the student newspaper "Brig", and sending job applications. For my dissertation it was essential to visit archives in other cities for several days. This meant that I had to isolate a week where I did not have a major deadline due within 5 days minimum of returning and it also could not be the newspaper editing week at the end of the month. As a result I was able to isolate some time slots in September and make all of the essential transport and accommodation arrangements.

Who do I need to work with?

You have to consider their availability, and once you've established a meeting time you do not have to worry about when to meet that person. Therefore, you can focus on fewer tasks in the rest of your time.

For example, as I mentioned in a previous article (insert link), it is always a good idea to be prepared for working on other tasks if necessary. This is particularly true if you are expecting to work with other people. When I was preparing to work on a group project at University I would always bring other work with me so I would not waste time if my partners could not make it on time.

How can I do this work?

One of the absolute cardinal rules of effective time management is that you assign your most difficult tasks to your most productive working hours. If a task requires research then you have to be able to focus more to complete it.

For example, I am a morning person, so when I have serious deadlines I focus on getting to sleep early at night so that I can wake up early. I would assign any complicated or creatively challenging tasks for first thing the next morning and assign simpler laborious tasks for the late afternoon and night time.

The perfect colour coding and sticky labels system for students

Colour coding was a saving grace for dealing with large amounts of reading.

I will say from experience that one of the most stressful aspects of reading for an essay is when you forget which source a particular piece of evidence and what page it is in.

Colour coding can become a mess, if your strategy is to colour anything that could possibly be relevant without assigning particular colours to particular purpose them you will get lost.

However, if you follow the simple strategy outlined in this blog post then you will be fine.

Itinerary

You will need some useful stationary to complete this task. Ideally make sure that you have the same variation of colours for each of these types of stationary.

Small sticky labels (small enough to attach to the outside margin of a book)

OR coloured pens, you can decide based on whether you are willing to leave a permanent mark on the source paper.

Blank A4 paper.

Larger sticky labels, 'Post It' style

First Stage

If you are reading an article that you have printed then you can highlight individual pieces of text for a particular purpose (e.g. a particular sub-topic).

Alternatively, if you have borrowed a book from the library which you should not leave a mark on then you can put the small sticky label on the page, and next to the paragraph containing the relevant information. (Remember to remove the labels before returning the book).

Importantly, you must number each point that you highlight or each label that you stick in the margins, so that you can keep track of the points in the second stage.

Second Stage

Then you should take a blank piece of A4 paper and write the source title at the top. Take a larger square sticky label, write down the number of the point which you have given to the highlighted point, and then write out why the evidence is useful.

Make sure that the big sticky label is the same colour as the coloured pen (yellow in every example in this article) or small sticky labels which you have used to isolate the point in the source text.

Benefits of this system

Just like the 'Ideas Sheet', this system of colour coding is beneficial because it allows you to have all your best insights related to the evidence on a few pieces of paper. In turn this means that you can put them in a logical order, develop useful links between them, develop links with other evidence that you have noted from other sources using the same method, and then use these to help build a logical essay structure and coherent thread of argument.

Dealing With Notes to Find Information Easily

I had a gigantic folder containing all the paper notes from each of my dissertations. Also a mass of online notes which I never printed off. In any major assignment, it is critical to remain on top of the important information from your subject.

By piling notes on top of each other with no clear strategy for dealing with them you are setting yourself an extra arduous and completely unnecessary task.

This chapter will outline the specific steps that I took to clear the clutter from my notes, and which I feel contributed significantly to obtaining my first-class degree.

Exams

Since exams are supposed to cover everything that you have done so far in your course it is necessary to start breaking down the essential points from each week's lectures or seminars – ideally every week – before the end of term. By doing this you are not being faced with a daunting mountain of clutter, with a disappointing lack of coherence.

Take the notes for each week and use different highlighter pens to isolate the more important evidence, academics, and schools of thought. Then re-write them in a cohesive order from which you could build a stronger model answer when term ends and then final exam preparation begins.

Essays

As I have mentioned before my essay strategy used to be that I would research until I felt that I could build a plan with a cohesive argument. However, being a perfectionist I could never stop researching, and when I took my plan and tried to write out my essay I would always want to find more information from my massive pile of notes. This led to many stressful all night writing and editing sessions.

The key to managing essay notes is to build them into your essay as you go along. When you find an important piece of evidence or analysis in an academic source you should write it as you would if you were inserting it directly into your essay. Then if you find any pieces of evidence or analysis which you can connect to it you can then add them to the same paragraph in your notes directly. Even if you think you would need to change it when you cut and paste it into your essay, it will still make it easier to edit. It is also a fantastic way to overcome writer's block.

If you start your research with the most recent major source then you can map out the different schools of thought, and then read the following important texts by seniority and theme, so you can then establish an ideal structure for your essay.

Dissertations

For your dissertation, most of the rules for your essay still apply but in a considerably greater quantity. However there are strategies which you can use to overcome the extra work which is required to take control and prevent extreme clutter in your notes.

If you have a huge amount of evidence from certain major sources then it helps to have it in a linear order based on some logical timescale in the first place. From there you can:

Make a list of keywords at the top of the notes
When you conduct a keyword search by clicking ctrl + f on your keyboard you can locate every time when you have used it.

Number and date your pages
This is the most logical and time efficient way of locating a particular piece of evidence. If you are making a plan and using an ideas sheet and want to leave a reminder of where to find a particular piece of evidence then just leave the identifiable number with whatever extra identifiers you need (e.g. source name).

If you do use dates for cross-referencing then it helps to organise your notes by date. If you made notes on Word Documents then maybe include dates on the file name so that you can find it when you keyword search for documents on your File Explorer.

Above all else it is important that you adapt when you feel you need to. Add another identifier when and how you feel is necessary to keep your notes organised.

2

Beyond Uni.
Lifestyle, Fun,
Time management
and Job Interviews

Best research tactics for any job interview

Job interviews can be the stuff of nightmares. Thinking about what question the interviewer will ask? Will they blind side you? How will you react?

Research skills are critical to proving that you are the perfect employee. The best interviewee would – in theory – be able to start work on the day of the interview. They would know about the organisation's current challenges, the environment in which they operate, and the recent news coverage which is related to the organisation.

Very few employers want to hire someone who will have to take large amounts of paid time to learn before they can start their real work.

This chapter will describe how you should approach research for an organisation and how it will help you in any job interview.

Search current news

Depending on the size of an organisation, many important stories will be readily available online in the news and on the organisation's website and social media channels.

News about the company can be very helpful for answering general interview questions such as "What attracts you to our organisation?".

Make a list of the 5 most relevant individual news stories to your position, from across various media outlets, and write down in your own words why they influenced your decision to apply and how you can work effectively for them under the circumstances.

Isolate the key information

On the other hand, if you specify your department or the area of a company that you are applying for then you can avoid wasting time and direct your attention to the most vital information. Even a simple Google search with several keywords (e.g. "Company X Human Resources") can allow you to obtain access to the specific information that your role will demand.

To make it even more straightforward you can take the specific roles and responsibilities mentioned in the job description to minimise your searches.

By isolating the key information you can establish the key challenges and goals for your department and even provide some of your own insights. This will help a great deal when you are asked about how you are qualified for the specific position in the organisation.

For example, here are some cases from my own experience to give you some idea of where you should research key information.

- For my Corporate Social Responsibility job application I located the "Corporate Social Responsibility report 2015 – 2016" as well as news reports on specific social schemes sponsored by the company.
- For my digital media marketing job application, I examined the website to give positive insights on improving it's internal structure and user friendliness.

Contact the right people

If the information that you want to find out is not available online, then just contact the right person within the company.

Persistence is critical to good research, and making contact with the right people can be especially challenging.

In many large organisations there will have specific contact details for certain departments available online. However, even in a small organisation with an online presence you can find contact details for the whole organisation. If you use the general contact details then you can ask for a phone number or email address for someone who can provide more specific information. Even for a local organisation with no online presence, you can often find contact details using the Yellow Pages.

For example, when I went for a web editor position I wanted to find out what content management system they used, so I could provide more specific insights. After 20 minutes on hold and being switched between different departments I finally located a phone number. Then after calling I was switched through again and finally found someone who could tell me.

Persistence pays off!

Steps to take to ace any job interview

I remember the first time that I got a job interview. I was exhilarated ... and absolutely TERRIFIED!

Putting your life's achievements and your personal qualities on paper is very different from having them scrutinised in person by someone analysing your immediate answers, tone, and body language on the spot.

Had I known about these essential steps in advance I would have felt far more secure. Take a minute and equip yourself with the necessary steps for preparing for any job interview.

Prepare Basic Questions

In my first interview, it was the most basic questions that through me off guard. I had prepared really specific questions based on the job description, but when I was confronted with a general "why do you want to work for us?" my answer was confused, disordered, and did not include some of the best information. This was due to the fact that I had not memorised the job information in the order for such a broad question.

So always begin every job interview preparation with the same fundamental questions that you would ask of anyone joining your organisation:

- Why do you want for work for us?
- What do you think qualifies you for this position?
- Where do you see yourself in one year?

Prepare skill-specific questions

The skills-specific questions were critical to the success of my first interview even when I seemed confused when answering the basic questions.

If you are confused, then the first step should be to take a highlighter pen and colour over the essential responsibilities and skills described in the main text. Then simply rephrase the description of the responsibility as you would ask in a question.

The basic criteria for answering these questions is to follow the S.T.A.R. formula.

Situation – what was the context of the example (e.g. setting, your role);

Task – what was the job that had to be done, and why did it have to be done;

Actions Taken – what actions did you take to complete the task and resolve the situation, and why did you think that they were the correct actions to take;

Result – What was the immediate and (if necessary) long-term result of your actions?

Contact HR for answering criteria

For some large employers, there is a more precise and detailed answering criteria available online. Alternatively, if you cannot find one then you can phone up human resources and if you ask very nicely they might just direct you to its online location, or even email it to you.

Using this answering criteria it is possible to make more developed answers which perfectly fit what the employer wants to hear from you.

Mock interview

Even after all the preparation and research nothing matches the pressure of having to answer under pressure on the spot. Make sure you rehearse at least once with a close friend or relative.

Alternatively, if you are still a student, most universities will have a careers service that will offer you a mock interview appointment.

Prepare at least 2 constructive questions for the interviewer

The last question in every interview that I've ever had was whether I had any questions for them. But do not be tempted to sound smart or overly technical. Instead ask them constructive questions which show that you already thinking about how you will settle in and work well in the job from the day that you begin.

<u>Extra Tip</u>

My strategy for preparing thoroughly for exams could be useful in this context because you have to memorise information in a logical order and in separate scenarios, ideally using the **filing cabinet system** (Page 55).

Essential tasks the day before a job interview

The day before an interview, it always helped me to have a routine schedule to follow so that I would be efficient with time and not fret too much about things which I might have missed.

It is very easy to overthink your preparation and to work on it to the point where you are damaging your chances of working well in your job interview. So follow these essential tips and you will be set up well.

Review notes and job description

The most obvious starting point. Make sure that you know your qualifications for a job off by heart!

There are a number of ways that you can review you notes and job description so that you can safely rely on instinct when you into an interview.

I would always number the scenarios which I took note of, in order to easily break them down in my head – which in turn is critical for flexibility when the interviewer asks you an unexpected question.

Iron your clothes

First impressions are critical, and so appearance counts for a lot. Creases on your clothes give an immediate bad impression, because they are associated with disorganisation, uncleanliness, and a lack of care and attention.

I always iron my clothes the day before because I find ironing a relaxing activity, and I feel relaxed when I see them hanging up on my wardrobe, just waiting for me to step into with ease tomorrow.

Prepare everything that you will need

Make a small list of everything that you will need in order to deliver your interview and how you will get there and back.

If you need to give a presentation then make sure your computer is working well, and that you have backups of everything that you need on a pendrive and a cloud storage (e.g. OneDrive, GoogleDrive). If you have flashcards that you will use to remember vital information then set them aside so that they will not get lost with your other notes.

For getting to the interview, make sure that you know exactly where you are going and approximately how long it will take to get there. You should plan to get there with at least 30 minutes to spare. If you have an early interview during rush hour then be even more generous with time, giving yourself aiming to get there 45 minutes to 1 hour in advance.

Sleep Well

No employer wants to see you asleep at your desk at work! So if you come for an interview during the daytime and you look like you've been out on the town all night it will not give a good impression.

Besides good first impressions, you are more likely to give good answers to interview questions when you mind is well rested. You will be well equipped to remember important information for your answers and describe them with ease and confidence.

The recommended amount of sleep to get is between 7 and 9 hours, with 8 being the ideal number.

Prepare for Sleep

In order to get a good sleep to put you in the right shape for going to your interview, it is essential to prepare yourself the night before.

It is important to put your work away for an hour or two before you go to sleep, and relax your mind. Stay away from Facebook, Twitter, and Instagram, as it has been shown that social media can promote insecurity and anxiety which makes it harder for you to sleep. Likewise, do not watch anything with a lot of hard-hitting drama or intensity, because that will stimulate internal chatter and debate and leave you feeling restless.

The night before an interview I would brush my teeth and get everything ready for going to sleep around 8 or 9pm. To relax I would watch something funny for an hour and remove and internal conflict or chatter about my interview.

What everyone can learn from travelling and living in hostels

Hostelling has been a really eye opener in my last three holidays and visits to Europe.

Sleeping in a dorm with seven other travellers, sharing facilities and space was certainly a shock to someone used to living in his own room. There was no way to feel comfortable if you did not socialise with the other travellers. However, the forced socialising brought real benefits of its own.

It's inexpensive and unpretentious and forced me to adapt in a number of ways, which in turn, has allowed me to enjoy myself a great deal more.

If you enjoy company and friendship, but feel slightly nervous away from the people you know, then hostels are a perfect stimulant for socialising. Anyone who is experienced in hostelling will tell you that the mutual dependence when it comes to living side by side with the aim of exploring a new city will bring people together common experiences and diverse backgrounds.

Once my first hostel holiday to Budapest was over I saw the benefits in my day-to-day life. For example, when I went for a training course at WordCamp Manchester 2017 I found that my networking was improved by the ability to strike up small talk and build up to more relevant topic-related conversation. This was because I felt comfortable that whatever reservations I had in attending this unfamiliar event alone were shared by many others who were there as well.

Enjoy serendipity

As an obsessive planner this is a very strange choice for someone like me. However, there's no way to deny that the pleasure of the unexpected has been integral to my experience of hostels, especially if you meet someone who has been there a few days and can recommend things which you may not have heard about online or in your travel brochures. In Dublin, I had come to see the Guinness Storehouse and the Temple Bar district. But instead on the first day I went with two Venezuelan roommates to Croke Park, the spectacular 83,000 seat home of Ireland's two largest native sports: Gaelic football and hurling.

I appreciate an authentic piece of local culture in any destination, and that visit to Croke Park gave me an insight into a unique Irish cultural tradition in one of the most historic and beautiful sporting venues in the world.

High quality of relationships

Although you may only meet people in hostels for short periods of time I have found that people will go from 0 to 100 quite quickly. By this I mean that they will recognise your vulnerability as you recognise theirs. It is not an easy way to travel and the mutual struggle created a lot of empathy with other travellers in the cities where I visited. So people would be more willing to listen to your intimate concerns about your journey and I found that I genuinely wanted to get to know these people that I met.

Also, once you become comfortable with these people you will want to know as much about them in the short time that you are able to spend there. This means that the days will be more interesting and you might get further inspiration for travelling, especially if you are doing a sizable amount of travelling and you want to find places where you have contacts.

How running improved my academic performance

I think running is the best alone time that anyone can have

As I have mentioned in previous posts, I run at least twice every week, I have previously ran a 10K and a half-marathon, and I aim to finish a marathon in 2018. I have been running outdoors for exercise on and off since I was 15.

However, I would not class myself as a "runner" because that would be separating me from other people. The leap in standard needed for running in races is not as big as you think. In this post, I want to show all of you that taking some time out of my weekly schedule to go running has improved more than just my fitness.

Productivity

If you have worked long-hours on complex projects then you will know that willpower alone is insufficient for productivity. There will be periods where you feel severe mental block and stare blankly at the screen or a sheet of paper.

After about 30 minutes of mental block I would try and run for 30 minutes to divert my attention away from the task in hand. The physical stress which was brought on by the constant sitting down and critical thinking would be relieved by the running which made me physically tired while clearing my mental tiredness and confusion.

When I had finished my run I would be able to start the task again with the same state of mind that I had begun with in the morning. I could relax and see the steps which had to be taken with real mental clarity.

Creativity

The repetitiveness of running can manifest into boredom. This creates a major deterrent for people to start running and then keeping going out. However, I would like to tell you why the repetitiveness is a godsend anyone working on a creative project.

The repetitiveness of the movements and the plain thinking which runners engage in when they identify their route has the effect of clearing your mind of negativity around other parts of your work.

The mental clarity which I gained from running also allows creative breakthroughs to come through that would not have happened if I had stayed at my desk all that time.

Self-esteem

I cannot emphasise enough the boost which running and other exercise brings to your self-esteem. It does not just help your self-esteem by improving your physical appearance, but by giving you the feeling that you are doing something right. I always found that an hour or more of mental block can be detrimental to self-esteem, because it is just time wasted.

So if you take some time out when you are suffering from mental block you will get more throughout the whole day from the time that you have put into work, and also get your daily exercise completed.

Diet

In order to run well I had to force myself to adapt to a healthier diet. Running without energy is especially boring, so I got into the habit of eating a banana before each run. This had a knock on effect on my work life, because I saw the impact of healthy eating on my ability to think clearly while running. As a result I decided to bring bananas to the library instead of chocolate and other processed sugary food and drink.

So by wanting to run, I was also able to get into the habit of eating better food which has improved my overall health.

Moving back in with parents: How to avoid getting comfortable.

Like many graduates, I moved back home after completing my degree!
I have kept telling myself a number of reasons why this is acceptable right after graduating from University.

The best reasons so far have been

I am from Glasgow, which in of itself is a larger jobs market than Stirling, where I was studying for the past five years, so there is no point in staying away.

Until I get a steady, decent paying job, rent is a terrible and unnecessary drain on savings.

My best friend will be coming back to Scotland near to the end of the year so it would be good to wait until we could sort something out together.

However, the comforts of home with Mom and Dad can be all too tempting.

This article will guide you through the steps which I have taken to ensure that I do not become stuck in the comfort zone.

Difference between reasons and excuses for living with parents

For me personally, **reasons** equate to a justifiable factor which affects your personal situation and decisions. Alternatively, **excuses** equate to barriers which you give yourself in order to remain in your comfort zone.

Now, while some of the reasons for moving back into your parents' house are justifiable there is an inherent risk that you will not be motivated to change them. Here are some key steps to keeping yourself on the ball and moving forward:

1: Get used to dealing with awkward or unappealing tasks yourself

When I moved away from home for the first time I had to get used to dealing with numerous difficult or awkward tasks by myself. Whether it was simply tasks such as handling cleaning and cooking, to managing my time more strictly, I learned that embracing the task and taking control of it was better than allowing it to fester. Once I allowed a task to fester because it seems too difficult or awkward then the scale of it would grow inside my head until it had become impossibly overcomplicated.

Once you achieve mental clarity it is possible to break down many seemingly difficult or awkward tasks with remarkable ease. I have even begun meditating each morning.

2: Stick to a routine

To be successful at university and in work I believe that it is essential to take full control of your time. Accept that it is no one else's responsibility setting the steps for your success other than your own. This applies to your sleeping patterns, how you chose to spend the hours you spend awake, and how you pursue self-improvement in your life.

It is at this point that routine becomes critical. In my experience, my mental health and productivity were facilitated by the reliable repetitive actions which would immediately lead me on to complete the next task, rather than lying in a state of limbo waiting for something or someone to push me forward.

3: Set a condition for staying and for moving out

If you are telling yourself that you will definitely move out one day, it is a good idea to write out the circumstances under which you will live at home or move out.

If you have a good low or entry level job then work out what you would be paying in rent if you were not living at home. Then set yourself the goal of saving that amount of money – perhaps in a separate savings bank account – which you will be able to use for something useful in the long-term future, such as a down payment on a mortgage for a house.

#0062 - 040918 - C0 - 210/148/6 - PB - DID2295019